# HALF

## AND

# WHOLE

## A SOUND AND MUSIC NOTE PRIMER

 JEREMY WELLS  © 2022

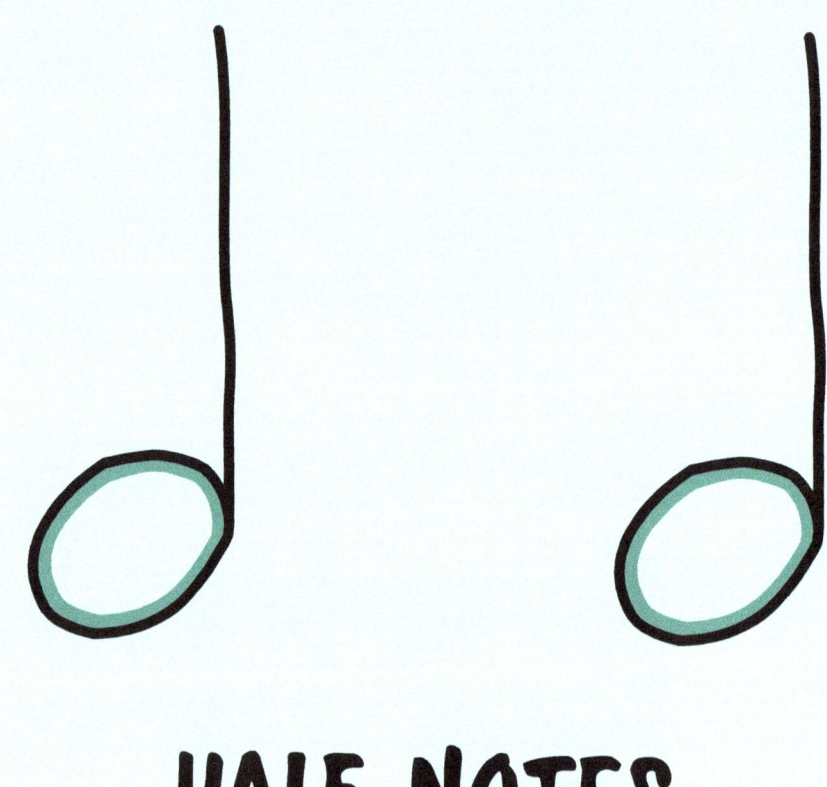

HALF NOTES

WHOLE NOTE

HALF RESTS

WHOLE REST

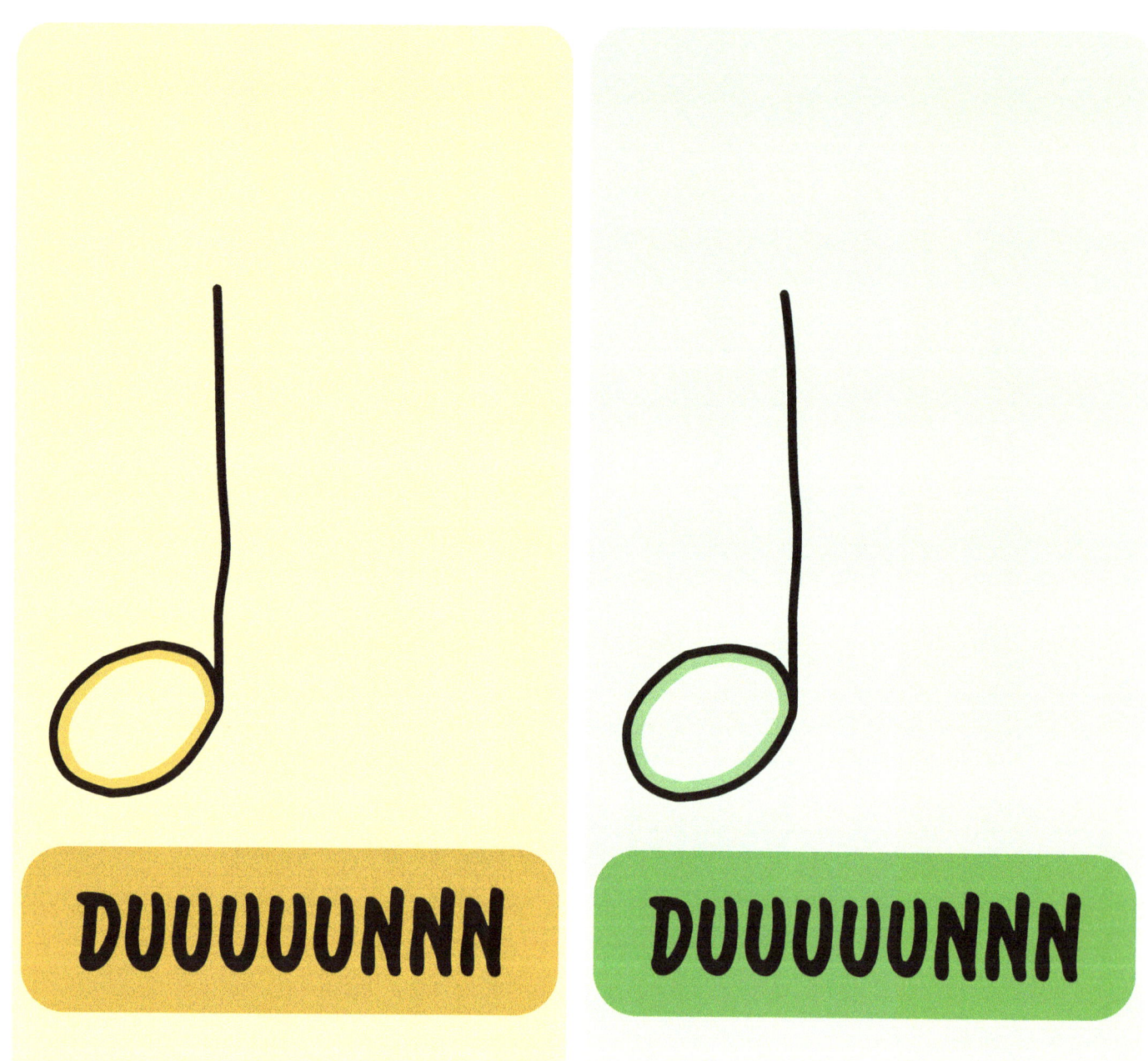

DAAAAAAAAAAAAAAAAAAAAAHH

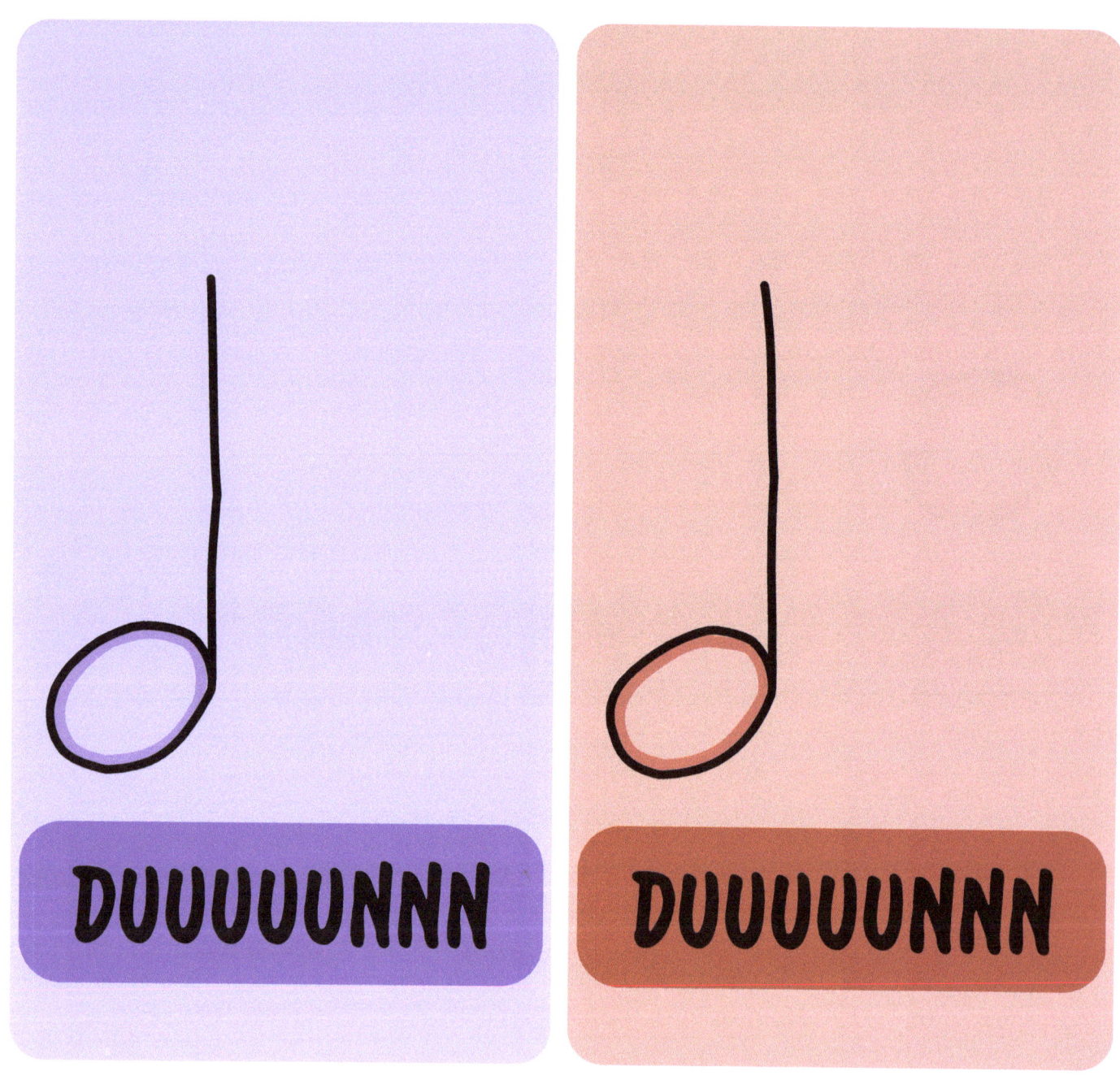

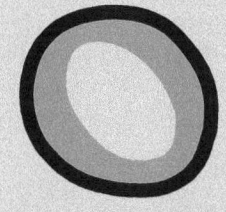

DEEEEEEEEEEEEEEEEEEEEEEEEEEEEEEE

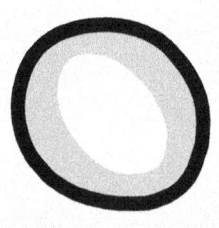

DAAAAAAAAAAAAAAAAAAAAAAAAY

DOOOOOOOO

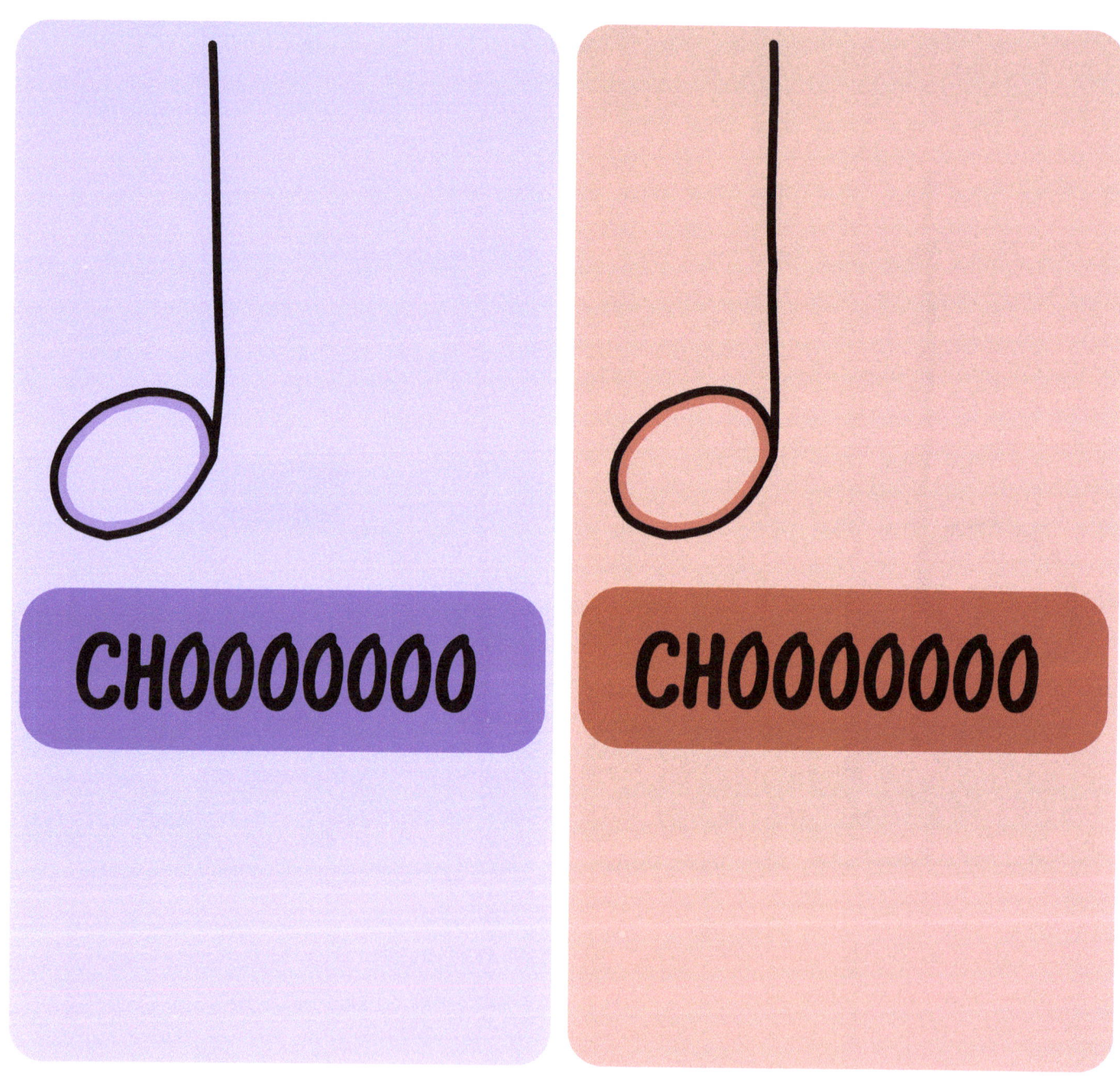

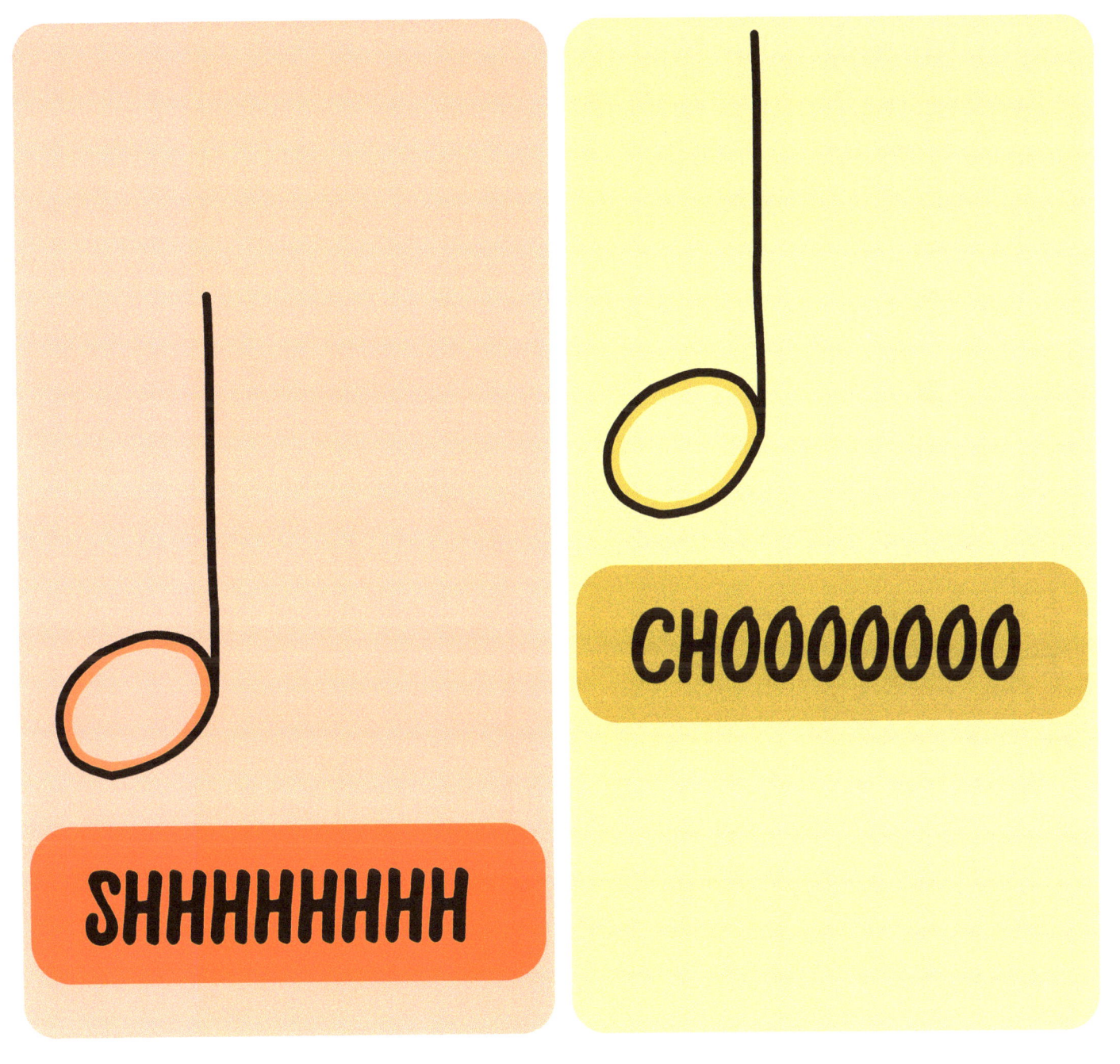

TEEEEEEEEE

TAAAAAAAAY

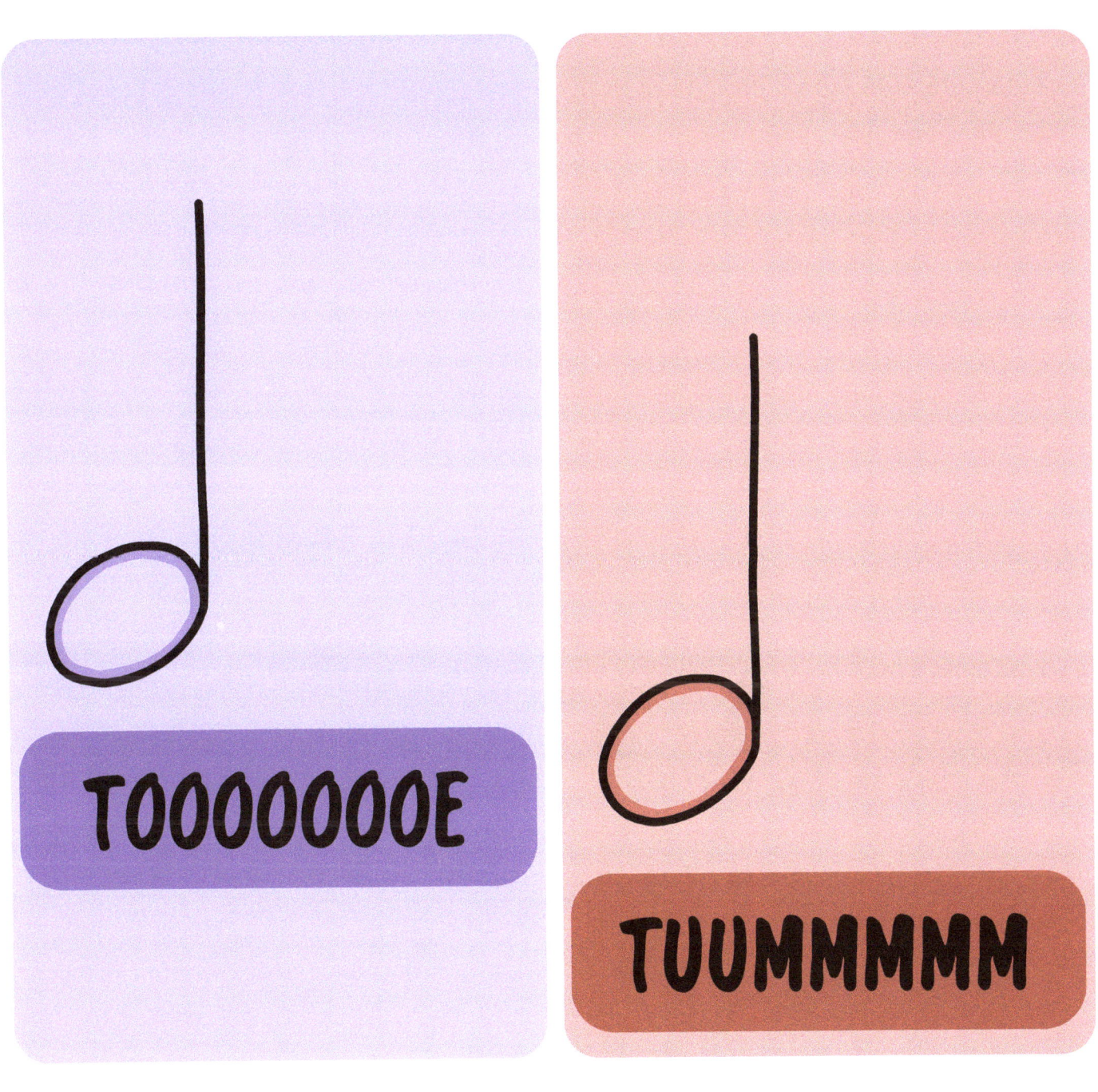

BOOOOOOOM

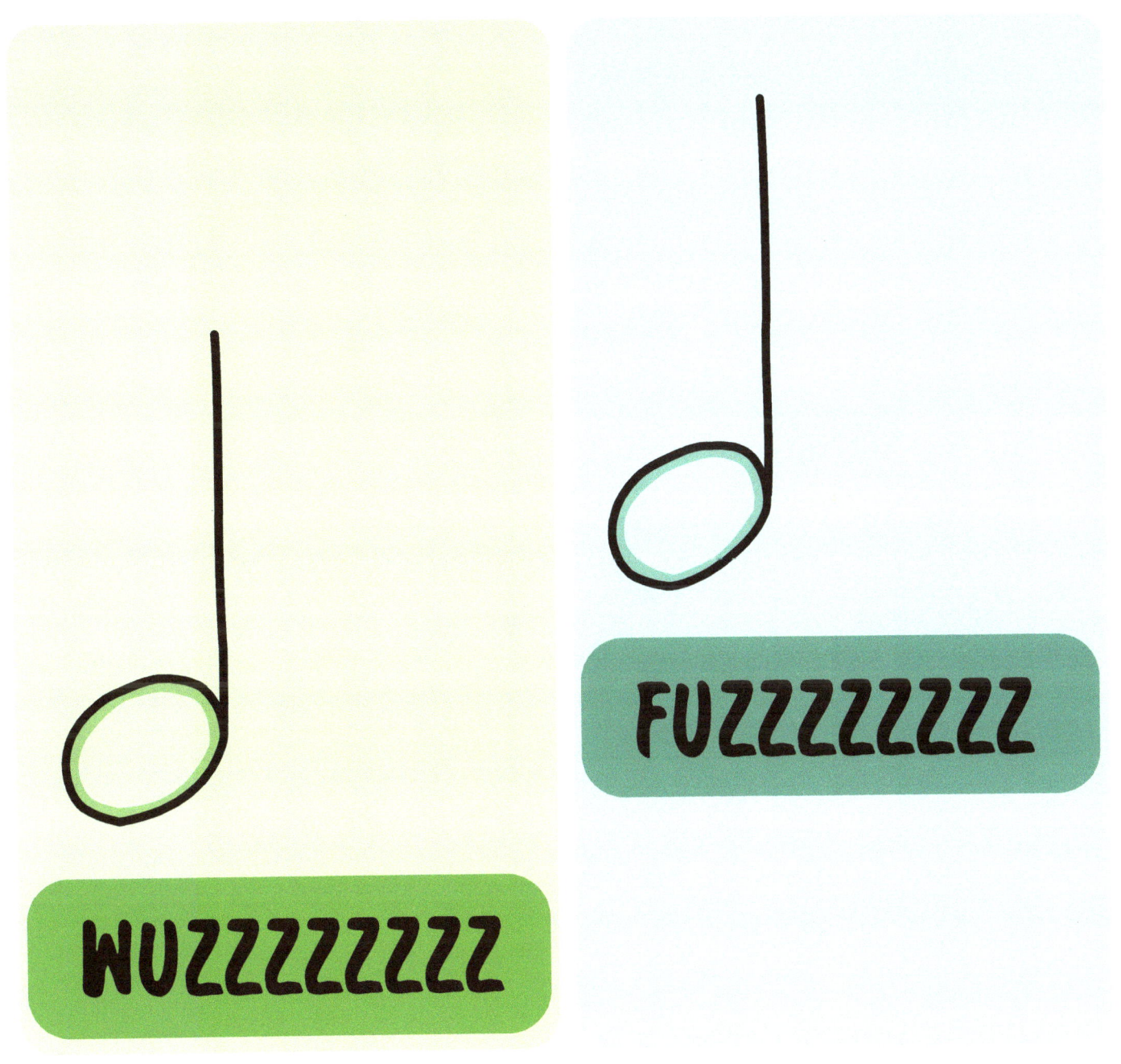

DOOOOOONG

DIIIIIIIIIING

AAAAAAAAAAAAHHHHHHHHHH H H
O

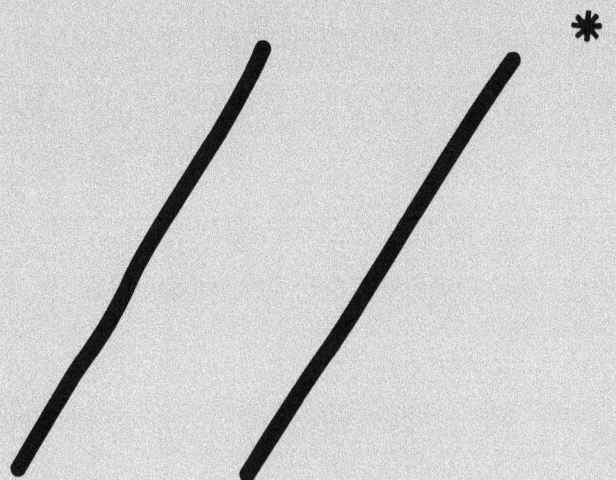

(. . WAIT FOR IT . . . WAIT FOR IT . . . AND . . )

*CESURA: BIG DRAMATIC PAUSE

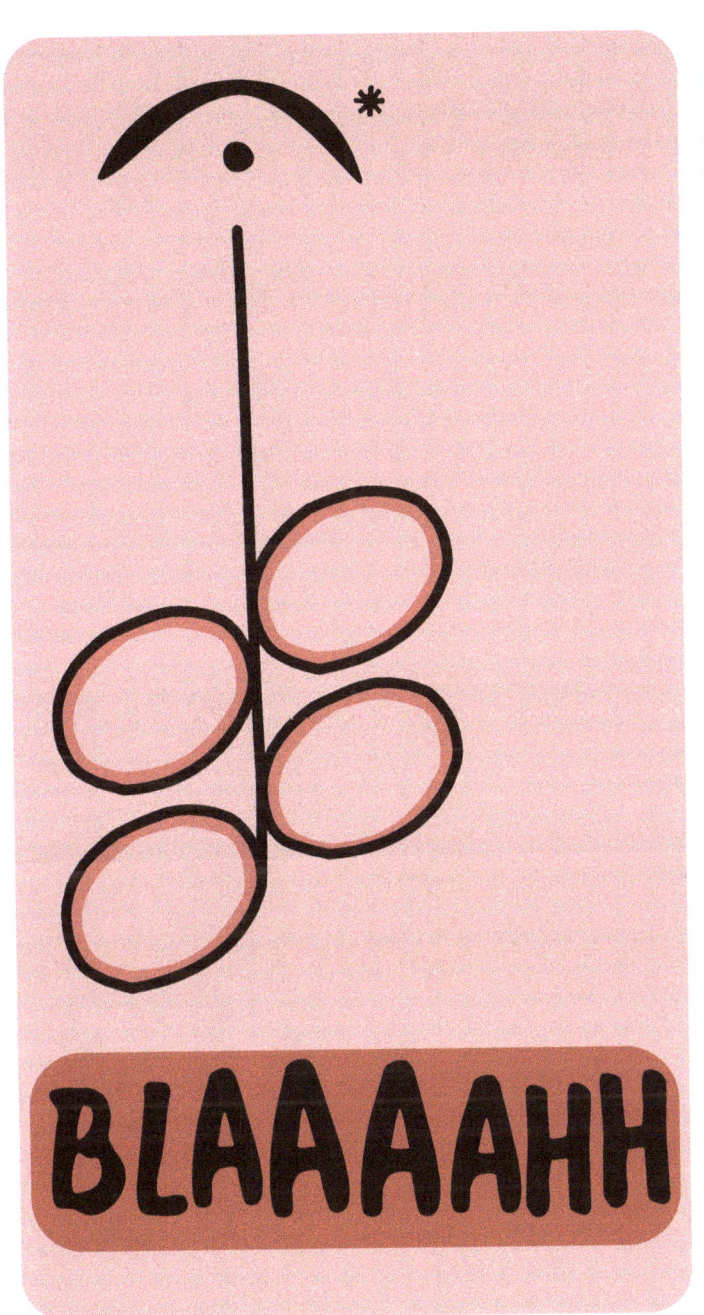

*FERMATA: SING AS LONG AS YOU LIKE

CLAP
CLAP
CLAP
CLAP
CLAP
CLAP
CLAP
CLAP
CLAP
CLAP
CLAP
YEEAAAHH
YEEAAAHH

CLAP
CLAP
CLAP
CLAP
CLAP
CLAP
CLAP
CLAP
CLAP
CLAP
CLAP
CLAP
CLAP
CLAP
YIPEEEEEE
YAHOOOOO